*To Robin manager of S and North DL areama from RJMac*

# THE MASKS

*Dear Robin I would appreciate your feedback on this Book cheers*

ISBN:9798828318582

## Mete Can Yumru

*8th of January 2024*

# IMPOSSIBLE LOVE

You look familiar, have I seen you before?

There are many words we have yet to speak.

Where the rain rises, and mountains peak.

Your eyes were gleaming, my heart was soar.

And when the minutes began to roar,

From now until forever more,

Where the forests turned into light before the end of a mile,

And faded away like the fire of the night.

Where the tears of a thousand lovers ran like the Nile.

There you have tried to wear my smile.

Your hands are small, mine are too big.

Where the ants became giants I have heard you speak:


'Love is a jewel we all seek,

Even if everything turns bleak.'


You said my lips tasted like the sweetest candy,

And I said yours tasted like the salt of the ocean.

Weren't we the ones who touched the sky?

And made the clouds rain when the summer was dry.

My tears evaporate each day on sun set,

And condensed to fall the next day.

There we marveled at the light of the night,

And we kissed until our lips ran dry.


You told me to let the sun rise and stars fall.


We were where the night and day were put to shreds.

And where a dream from my childhood threads,


I am here whenever you call,

You told me that love is not for all.


Mete Can Yumru

# SOMEONE ELSE

If she was hurt it was not me, it was

Someone else.


Whoever separated us it was not me, it was

Someone else.


Maybe now all is said and done,

There was a time not long ago when I was her one.


I have done my best, then be gone!

I can not believe who I have become.


Someone.


Mete Can Yumru

# WHAT CAN LIGHT DO IN THE HANDS OF MIDNIGHT?

What can light do in the hands of midnight?

Even when I know that she have blessed me with herself,

And when the last breath of the morning turns silent,

One of the cursed nights when my only company is myself,

I open my mouth to say only her name.

When another nameless hour approaches,

I wonder where she is, when darkness forms darker arches.

Without her I can't even walk with crutches.

And where we could have been if we stayed together,

Maybe then nothing else would matter.


Whereever I go I see her face.

And just when I lose the count of days.

I whisper her name again,

And I feel shocked to see she is still not with me.

Then I wonder while walking on the empty streets,

Where she is, where she has been, and where she will be.

I know that some day she will call me, she just might.

But what can light do in the hands of midnight?


Mete Can Yumru

# PIECES FELL

As I walked on the streets thinking of you,

The anger in me has suddenly grew,

The windows of the shops all shattered and,

Pieces fell.


Separation is shameful at best,

All those beautiful days together have passed,

The weeks have now turned to seconds and,

Pieces fell.


I remember a song you sang,

Clear in my head your voice rang,

Words were taken from sentences and,

Pieces fell.


Ever since the day you were gone,

It felt like even my last breath has drowned

My heart is torn to ashes, this must be hell,

Pieces fell.

Mete Can Yumru

# BLONDER

The sun is blonde, but you are blonder.

You are the light that leaks from my curtains,

And that sweet voice in the middle of the night,

Like the brightest moon with skin white,

The impersonification of lust,

How many full moons have passed?

Gold is gold even if you smear it with dust.


I am whole only with you.

To me only your yellow is true.


Shame on the days we squander!

The sun is blonde, but you are blonder.


Mete Can Yumru

# IN LOVE

Notice how everything seems so much more beautiful,

The earth gives sweeter fruits, with love everything is plentiful.

Let us celebrate with love indeed we feel more alive.

Rejoice my love, we are in love.


There is very little left until the summer knocks on our door,

I will never leave you, not this summer not ever after, I swore.

The horizon is our future, and soon we will arrive,

Be patient my love, we are in love.


Troubles will only come and go,

If we stick together there is only bliss, nothing more.

We have been everywhere, everything we saw,

We belong together my love, we are in love.


Like a fabric our love grows, woven

A lover's heart is hard to fix once it is broken.

I promise, I will be more gentle from now,

Rejoice my love, we are in love.


Mete Can Yumru

# BEAUTIFUL

I give you all the colors and the sunset's red,

And a humble lover's heart please do not dread.

Without you my heart endlessly suffers,

I give you the silver winters and golden summers.

My beautiful let us see it through,

Please do not leave me, I love you.


Mete Can Yumru

# DRUNKARD

Do you know she is your true love?

I do.

Do you sometimes take her for granted?

I do.

And then comfort her when she is sad?

I do.

Do you do everything you can to get her back?

I do.

Do you take her to be your lawfully wedded wife?

I do.

My beautiful, my only wish was to marry you.

I drank two rivers of wine,

If I didn't, I was going to lose my mind.


Mete Can Yumru

# ONE

Like a flower the moon brings,

Like a song a bird sings,

Like our dreams for tomorrow,

Like rejoicing after great sorrow,


Like drinking water from a fountain,

Like shouting to the sky on top of a mountain,

Like a cool breeze on a hot summer's day,

Like a debt you never have to pay,


Like the sun that shines at night,

Like truly knowing what is right,

Like watching the oceans burn,

Like a lover you thought would never return,


Like starting over at an old age,

Like a curious child turning a book's page,

Like a long desired rain needed for crops,

Like a few trees sprinkled on hilltops,


Voice peaceful like a mother's lullaby,

Always caring with a watchful eye,

Eyes gleaming like the brightest day,

Days like clay melting away.


Far away but close as she has ever have been,

And more beautiful than anything I mean.

I do not know what else can be done?

She is all my dreams become one.


Mete Can Yumru

# TWO

Your hair is wavy like windy tides,

I am no longer watching you on the sides.

Beneath the blue skies we are together, me and you,

One is no longer better than two.


We are not alone you and I, we work in doubles

Your hands write healing to all troubles,

We must not waste time, let us mingle,

Being a couple is so much better than being single.


Let us stop this game of hit and run,

We have each other to lean on,

I will make you happy, you are fun,

Two of us is always better than one.


Mete Can Yumru

# CHILDREN OF LOVE

Hunger,

Poverty,

War,

All dangerous plagues of today and tomorrow.


Red,

White,

Black,

We are all human for god's sake.


If you can not find the courage,

Make it summon.

In the end we all have something in common.


Let go of your anger,

We are all in this together.

What are you fighting for?

We all walk towards the same door.

We all share the same sky above,

And we are all children of love.


Mete Can Yumru

# GHOSTS IN THE NIGHT

Look you see the world is still turning.

For some love is nothing but games,

It is true they have eaten fire and swallowed flames,

So why is it that only those in love are burning?


It is hard to cope with break-up and loss, admit it.

Ask all the souls who has been through it.

It is hard on the body, the mind, spirit.

But we must heal as fast as we commit ourselves to healing.


There are millions of lovers on the planet,

Millions seeking love, finding it, cherishing it, losing it,

A circle that keeps spinning around,

Breaking and reforming, the ends finding a new beginning.

And beginnings ending.


It starts with denial, wondering has it really happened?

Am I really apart from my significant other?

Is it really over?

Perhaps then a roaring rage kicks in,

Tears flow, tears of love,

Or perhaps not even tears, just nothing.

Has this really happened, is it over?


The shining stars in the skies, heed us(lovers)!

Heed us(lovers), the ghosts in the night!


Mete Can Yumru

# FROM THE BEGINNING

Here I sit all alone,

I, Mete, newly reborn,


But since we have already been there,

I have a love story to share.


A story of love not sinning,

Shall we start from the beginning?


A house in a town where with rain rivers rise,

And the valley looks at the hills and sighs.

A town that lies between York and Newcastle,

We hit it off from the start without hassle.


My studies are completed, yours just start,

I knew you would always possess a throne in my heart,

You study hard with your glasses, I write,

It is like we are meant together, we never fight.

You have me my love, you are not alone,

Your hands reach quickly on your cell phone,

A rose on a mountain, untouched,

Even the peaks are not enough, our love is such.


Your face is so etched in my mind, it is true,

I do not even have to look to see you.


We are just beginning we are not done,

On a bed that was made for one.


A story of love not sinning,

Shall we start from the beginning?


Mete Can Yumru

# SEPARATION

You said it is your time to leave,

What will I do without you in Edinburgh?

It has been a year time flew by so fast,

It was only yesterday we started on our journey,

The exams were going to start last week.

But now you say the time has come to say goodbye.

And it is time to go home.

You will go far away, out of speech, out of sight.

It is our last night together and we do not sleep much.

We savor each moment until sleep takes us.

We were going to grow old in each others arms.

Good night baby, good night.


We tell each other we will visit often,

And we will talk often,

Long distance is hard.

I am sorry I could not come to you,

We tell each other this is not the end.

Far away, out of speech, out of sight.

Good night baby, good night.


Mete Can Yumru

# REUNION

You are just as I remember,

It is like you never left and this December,

We are together again in the city of seven hills,

You can do whatever you want to me as you please.


We talked for months before you arrived,

It is like you never left,

We are in a hotel,

In a room overlooking bosphorus,

This city is of fifteen million,

Spread upon the hills,

This city is where Asia and Europe meets.

And we meet here too.


No longer we stand apart,

We are a couple sharing an immigrant heart.

We have a lot to discuss,

And we are sure no distance can break us.

In the morning we listen to saz,

In Sultanahmet we have kofte piyaz.

In the afternoon we visit the museums and mosques,

And at night we are again in each others's arms.


I show you my home, you meet my parents,

The future is bright together.

Our love again is kindled,

Once we get married we can live in England.


It is time for her to take leave for home again,

To her home in the far east,

To me home is where my heart is.

At the airport she cries,

Tears start falling from her eyes.


I have a bad feeling about this do not go,

Stay with me.


Mete Can Yumru

# TOMORROW

She is swept away from me in an instant but,

Tomorrow is not.


Cherish the memories you are left with,

Enjoy your life, know when to let go.

Do not dwell any longer, do not mind it,

Because whoever seeks love again will find it.


Mete Can Yumru

# ANOTHER LOVE TO LIVE

There is another love, I promise,

When you lie down on your bed, and suddenly sadness takes over,

And just when you think it is over,

You will realize that you have yet another love to live.


Do not lose hope, this is not the end,

Put your head high, do not bend,

Love is not far, it is right around the corner,

You have yet another love to live.


Autumn is here, the trees begin to shed their leaves,

And their leaves fall beneath your feet,

Perhaps you are in a park, walking, to get thoughts in order,

And their leaves fall beneath your feet,

Perhaps like your thoughts your heart bleeds.

Remember then, it is not over.

Dry your tears, you have shed them enough,

Remember the days that you have smiled.

Love is not far away, it is just around the corner,

This is not the time for sadness but a time for cheer,

Like after a rain in summer, your heart is now clear.


Leaves fall beneath your feet,

I can carry you if you feel tired.

You can achieve everything by yourself,

But if you seek me, I am as close as your heart.


You are full of life, a woman, beauty itself,

You are not alone, if you need it there is always help.


Remember without you life can not exist,

Without you no one can exist.


You are the center of love,

You are the center of life.

Beautiful, you are everything.

Put me inside your pocket,

And keep me,

As a memory.


Move on if you must, but before that forgive,

You have yet another love to live.


Mete Can Yumru

# LIFE IS PRECIOUS

Life is so beautiful,

Like a grain of sand, a rain drop,

I wish nobody's heart ever stopped.


Life is a gift,

Live it.


Mete Can Yumru

# ETERNAL

Oh Lord, Almighty, High,

By your grace lovers may never die.


Mete Can Yumru

# SWAN

Where are the swans on the lake?

Your love in my heart, no one can shake.

Where are the trees, the mountains, the sun?

There are no others, there is but only one.

Where is that smile, that enlightens my soul?

Why are the smells now feel so foul?

Where is that bread we shared?

Where is that taste?, no one could have me prepared.

And the soup I made you when you were sick?

All I am now is stone, marble and brick.

Why are you shaking? Are you cold?

My heart is now a trinket no one has ever sold.

Where is that song, at the middle of the night?

When I lie awake to a magnificent sight.

Is this a love no one can behold?

Perhaps we fight again, it never gets old.

I still love you, if anyone knew…

Maybe now is the time to begin anew.

Mete Can Yumru

# SHE CRIED LIKE IT RAINS

She said she waits for it to rain before she cries,

Because noone can tell you cry when it rains.

It is like she spread her smile to everyone,

She gave it freely for everyone to share,

To her family, to her friends, to me.

But her tears belonged only to her,It seemed.

She did not like to share her sorrow with anyone.

Neither with her friends, nor with her family, nor me.

Or maybe I just could not tell when she cried.

As she only cries when it rains.

And maybe I could not distinguish her tears from rain drops.


One day It did not rain,

From sorrow no one gains,

And she cried like it rains.


Mete Can Yumru

# THE SUN

You are like the sun,

Burning with passion, spreading light to everywhere and everyone,

Alone in the cold, endless darkness,

Providing hope and warmth to everyone.

I orbit around you a lonely planet,

Moving in circles, not close enough but not far away either.

Never coming together with you, but constantly loving you.

And yearning for your touch.

I know one day we will unite,

And we will never separate from each other again.

Without you, I am alone.

Without me, you are alone.


At least we have each other.


Mete Can Yumru

# BECAUSE OF LOVE

Why do we fall?

Because of love.

Why do we rise?

Because of love.

Love, love, love.


Mete Can Yumru

# SCARS WILL HEAL

Your scars will heal,

Whether they are made by me or others,

I will kiss them one by one,

And make you well again.

I am not talking about scars in your body,

But in your soul.

You know the scars you carry within your soul always,

The ones that are hard to carry, those that bring you pain.

Learn to love your scars first so we can heal them together.

For those scars are remnants of the battles you have fought,

And won.

I will kiss them one by one,

And make you well again.

There is a place where there are no scars, I do not know where,

Together, we will go there.


Mete Can Yumru

# PURE OF HEART

I would do anything to make you smile,

Same as you would do anything to make me smile.

I know you love me so.

But you are much more than that.

You do your best to make everyone smile.

Because you are pure of heart.

This is why I love you,

And why I will always love you.


Whatever you touch, the smiles you bring,

Because of your pure heart, love will spring.


Mete Can Yumru

# BABY, IT'S OK

I didn't mean to hurt you,

I didn't mean to make you cry.

No matter what happens, no matter whay they say.

I love you baby, It's ok.


I want to make you happy,

I want to give you joy.

Should it be otherwise, with a pierced heart I will pay.

I love you baby, It's ok.


Mete Can Yumru

# ANGEL

The day that I met you

Is the day that I truly began to live.

What would an angel like you do with a human?

You have left your wings and decided to live on Earth,

With a creature like me,

Flawed,

Broken,

Dark.

You have brought your sweet voice from heaven,

That echoes in my ears like the most beautiful music.

And I do my best to make sure you have no regrets,

Because It would be a shame for an angel to feel regret.


Mete Can Yumru

# THE TIDE

No one can that easily turn the tide,

Relax baby, It is all right.


Mete Can Yumru

# OUR SONG

Remember our song?

The way we danced to it,
And the way we made love afterwards.

I want those days back.

Mete Can Yumru

# LOVE UNTAMED

Ours is a love untamed,

We live everything to the limit,

We kiss fiercely and we make love fiercely,

We live an unbalanced life,

We stay up all night together,

Than we sleep in the morning.

There are no rules in our lives.

Ours is a love untamed.

A love

Untamed


Mete Can Yumru

# START AGAIN

We break up,

Then we start again,

We break up,

Then we start again.

We could not solve our own riddle.

I hope there is a more stable future ahead.

We do not know where we are headed, but we are on a train.

We break up,

Then we start again.


Mete Can Yumru

# Long Distance Relationship

Long distance relationship is hard,

I can not go with you,

You can not stay with me.

We both want to stay with each other.

But we can not.

Now distance separate us,

Now we talk on the phone or chat over computer.

Remember I am one call away.

We had a good time together.

We have done many things together.

We were happy together.

When you are sad, when you are angry,

When you are happy, when you are filled with joy.

Whenever you want call me.

Because remember I am one call away.


Mete Can Yumru

# LEAVES FALL

Leaves fall,

Leaves fall because you have left.

I am stepping on the leaves, remembering a time not long ago.

I am remembering our time together.

Leaves fall.


Mete Can Yumru

# YOU ARE MINE TONIGHT

You are mine tonight,

Like two rain drops yearning for each other,

We will make love,

Like there is no tomorrow,

We will make love,

Remember,

You are mine tonight.


Mete Can Yumru

# SUNNY DAYS

I never meant to hurt you my love,

I only wanted sunny days for us,

I know still happy days are ahead,

Difficult days behind.

I never meant to hurt you my love.


After all these years,

I will heal your heart and remove your tears.


Mete Can Yumru

# I PROMISE

It was a gentle night,

The soft wind breezed through the roof,

We were in our room together,

Naked inside the bed,

We said we loved each other.

I promise I will always look upon you the way I do now,

I promise we will be happy.


Mete Can Yumru

# YOUR KISS

I yearn for your kiss baby, I yearn for your kiss,

I get out of bed in the morning and I go to work,

I brush my teeth and do the choires and so on.

Without you I am just a shell, all alone,

Moving on with my life just like a drone.

In the morning, in the afternoon, in the evening.

I yearn for your kiss baby, I yearn for your kiss.


Mete Can Yumru

# ONE DAY

Maybe one day,

I will hold your hands,

Again.


Mete Can Yumru

# THE BIRD THAT FLEW

I try to catch,

The bird that flew.


The bird that flew,

Is you.


Mete Can Yumru

# NOTHING

When you asked me 'What is wrong?'

I replied: 'Nothing.'

Nothing is easy.

It is easy to destroy but very hard to create,

A future, a bright future for the both of us.

So we can dwell in it,

Together.


Mete Can Yumru

# ALWAYS

I long for you,
Always.

Mete Can Yumru

# SEEKING LOVE

If you are seeking love I am here,

It will be like a walk in the park,

We will get along really well,
And we will love each other forever.

If you are seeking love I am here.

Mete Can Yumru

# FLOWER

Leave behind you all the gloom,

You are a flower, flowers bloom.


Mete Can Yumru

# PRINCE ISLAND

We can go to the islands bring your warm heart,

We can feed the birds on the ship,

The birds are so much like you,

They too have wings to carry them towards their dreams.

I left my heart on Prince Island,

I left my heart with you.


Mete Can Yumru

# BURNING

I am burning with the fire of your love,

Whereever I turn,

My side close to your fire burns.

I remember our time together,

Then I sit next to my chimney,

And pour some wine inside the glass,

I put wood inside the chimney and I realize,

Whereever I turn,

I am burning.


Mete Can Yumru

# THANK YOU

How can I express my gratitude?

You have been with me when everyone else left me,

To my own troubles and concerns,

Whatever happened you were there for me.

You were there for me when I needed your love,

You were there for me when I needed your smile.

I want to be with you,

And be with you for all time.


You are in everything I do,

What can I say? Thank you.


Mete Can Yumru

# THE GIRL ON THE TRAIN

You look very sad,

We are getting closer to the next stop,

Maybe next stop is your stop.

You play with your phone,

Then you start staring at emptiness.

Who are you thinking about?

I feel like you are an interesting person.

Perhaps your boyfriend left you.

Maybe you are going through some family issues.

My god, you are so beautiful.


Who knows what you are upto?

The girl on the train I wish I knew you.


Mete Can Yumru

# CRYING

Why are you crying?
Look we are happy,
We don't have any problems.
We have each other.
I am trying to create an utopia for you,
A fairy tale.
We have each other,
To cherish and to linger in the moments together,
Then why are you crying?

Mete Can Yumru

# I STILL LOVE YOU

I no longer remember,
How long has it been?
Since I last glided my fingers through your hair,
Since I last kissed you?
Not too long ago we were together.
And I loved you so much.
I still love you.

Mete Can Yumru

# TRUE LOVE

No matter how much time passes,
No matter how many heart breaks you experience,
No matter what love throws at you,
No matter how many times your love is tested,
True love never dies.

Mete Can Yumru

# WHAT KIND OF A GIRL

Life is like a blank canvas,

Whatever you draw on it that is your life.

This is the summary of life.


Whoever sees me notices immediately,

That I have been touched by love and loss thereafter.

What kind of a girl was she?

With the wind on her back and lies in her mouth.


Mete Can Yumru

# ONE AND ONLY

Whoever passes by, let them know us like this

You are the sunshine on my window, and the fog at my doorstep,

You know I can never let you go.

You are my one and only,

A single look from you is worth a thousand life times.

Mete Can Yumru

# POEM FOR THAT GIRL

I remained silent and I became all ears to the cries of hope,
And a black cat was scratching my ears,
When I have first felt on my forehead, the warm happiness of
the wind,
Suddenly, I felt an iron blitz in my veins.

I was in my room one day, silent and in the darkness,
If I hit the walls with my head the walls would break,
She was always in my heart,
And I knew she would remember me.

Mete Can Yumru

# A DAY WILL COME

We hope to say ' A day will come…'
Perhaps a day will come,
When thorns of roses get sharpened,
Instead of knives
Hopelessness is left behind somewhere far away,
Because to love is much better than to hate,
And the rising sun gets noticed by everyone.
A day will come when everything falls silent except the sound
of one's lover,
Like a deep music in our ears, life is colored by the voice of the
lover, humming like the most beautiful bird,
Loneliness will one day be forgotten.
And a day will come when love will be found.

Mete Can Yumru

# TRYING TO LOVE

Garlic is so tasty,
They say It makes you smell bad,
But what do they know?

Time is a beautiful thing,
'It is bad' they say, 'It makes you grow old'
But we leave our youths because we know we will grow old.

How beautiful it is to remain silent,
They force us to speak most of the time,
But sometimes the best thing to do is to remain silent and to cry quietly,
Because no life ends without a big smile.

How beautiful it is to love,
Maybe some could not love or refused to love,
Maybe they were afraid to love,
Alas, they could not love.

At least let me try.
Let us try.

Mete Can Yumru

# THE MASKS

I knew a tongue twister, I forgot it.

There was hatred in me, now It is gone from my soul.

There was more life in me, now that is gone too.


I always watched the theatre of life from behind the scenes,

I cried while the actors and actresses laughed.

What else could I do? They were all wearing masks.


They sold masks for cheap, two bucks,

I thought I should buy one, I woudn't wear It if I didn't like it,

I still can't take it off, It hardly fit me anyways.

The rebel in me was finally put to rest.


Many rain came fell upon the theatre,

Our eyes became dry, our cheeks became wet.

The chairs got cleaned, but the people were stained.

How many souls were sharpened by hatred?

How many times they have tried, they pierced our faces but,

They could not pierce our souls.


Perhaps we can become actors and actresses one day,

And we can make everyone forget about all the masks.


Mete Can Yumru

# KISS HER LIKE THAT

When I am happy, when I am sad,

When I am anything I want to kiss her like that.


Like a river meets the sea,

A dream, should It ever be,

Like drinking in haste a morning tea,

I must say I want to kiss her like that.


Like a raindrop kisses the grass,

Like a drummer hits the bass,

Like I was and I always will be, mad,

My god please let me kiss her like that.


Mete Can Yumru

# NIGHTS

I feel more free at night,
My hands are shaking, there is a twitch on my right eye,
The sun enters my room, the curtains can not hold the sun,
You see, the mornings cover the nights.

It is morning again things are happening outside,
Some people go to work, the shirts are ironed,
I feel more free at night,
The kids play hide and seek, the stars are hiding,
You see the mornings cover the nights,

Know this mornings, if I am silent it is because I am tired,
Nights I love you, please wake me up.

Mete Can Yumru

# ABOUT THE AUTHOR

Mete Can Yumru is a well-accomplished Engineer and Designer with a Bachelor's Degree in Industrial Engineering from Purdue University. He worked in the private sector for a bit before deciding to further his studies by completing a Master's in Design and Operations Engineering.

Mete has always loved to write. Ever since his early childhood, all he wanted to do was write and write whatever came to his mind. As an engineer, he enjoys analyzing everything and following a methodical approach to whatever he does. He uses his past experiences to put together useful advice along with easy-to-follow instructions so that you can get stuff done quicker.

As a writer, on the other hand, Mete has tried his hand at many different niches. From Mediterranean cookbooks, to financial books about the stock market and business, to poetry. Mete wants to share his talents and knowledge with the world and only hopes that you're able to learn something and enjoy his writing.

If you're interested in reading more of Mete's works then you can check out, www.amazon.com/author/metecanyumru , where all his works are published and ready to be enjoyed. Lastly, Mete wants you to know to always chase your dreams!

Please check the following link if you wish to buy more of my books.

http://www.amazon.com/author/metecanyumru

Printed in Great Britain
by Amazon

27204989R00046